Oz Hardwick

To Liz,

Very best wishes,

A CENSUS OF PRECONCEPTIONS

SV

SurVision Books

First published in 2022 by
SurVision Books
Dublin, Ireland
Reggio di Calabria, Italy
www.survisionmagazine.com

ISBN: 978-1-912963-38-6

This is dedicated, with huge thanks, to the poems' first readers from the Prose Poetry Project, and to those who have nodded and smiled along the way.

Acknowledgements

Grateful acknowledgement is made to the editors of the following, in which some of these poems, or versions of them, originally appeared:

192, Abergavenny Small Press Literary Journal, Abridged, Burrow, CC&D, Confluence, The Crank, Dreich, The High Window, HQ, HUSK, Ink, Sweat & Tears, International Times, Inverse, Lothlorien Poetry Journal, Meniscus, Northern Gravy, Parliament Literary Journal, Prole, Raven Cage, Stride, SurVision, Unbroken, Untitled: Voices, Up!, Westerly, The Wine Cellar, and the anthologies, *Despite Knowing: Poems on Addiction (2021), Emanations: When a Planet was a Planet (2021),* and *Silver Birch: I am Still Waiting (2021).*

"The Museum of Silence" won the Waltraud Field International Poetry Competition 2021, "Population: 0" won third prize in the MONO Poetry Competition 2021, and "Debrief" was longlisted for the AUB International Poetry Prize 2021.

CONTENTS

Awayday

With hands like candle stubs, I ease down the zip between now and never, and see a street in a city I recognise from movies. It's that city where serious towers bend clouds into animals like balloons at kids' parties; that city where the streets stream with scooters and yellow taxis. Sidewalks steam in the midday sun and the scuzz of sizzling meat nudges through like the unknown hero returning from a myth in the making. There's a kiosk selling scratch cards and I hand over a fistful of loose change that changes into a flight of neon dragonflies. Everyone's a winner here and I'm handed a second hand second chance at the split second I step through the slit between now and never. The zip sticks and I'm in a film I've never seen before, that rips before anything of consequence occurs. It's never been easy and now's not the time to be taking risks, but I'm tempted to close my eyes and stroll into endless traffic.

At the City Gates

When the city gates open, dreams flood out, like dockers on bicycles when the four o'clock siren sings freedom, oiled chains whirring like bees. It's been an age since anything worked, but there are grooves worn in blistered tarmac that you can see if you kick away the residue from the last high tide, and when you drop the needle the whole world spins like a charity shop album, playing a song everyone danced to when you were a teenager, though not by the original artist. There are still ships that come and go at night, freighting the Moon from far off ports, but you have only seen their glow, heard their crews calling in dead languages. When the city gates close, memories press their faces to the bars, each one familiar from wartime photographs, each one singing a familiar song to a tune that you don't recognise.

After Class

Magpies carry their own expectations, their privileged numerology and opportunistic grabs for all that glisters. So, when I meet one in that narrow alley between the school and the plastic works, I greet him with the respect he demands, doffing my flat cap as I slip my ringed fingers out of sight and into my threadbare pockets. Up close, his black wings are a shimmering slick of spilt oil, with all the colours of a bruised eye; his white is a flashbulb in a police station, framing the blame on a hapless stooge. He cocks his head, commands my sorrow, and cackles at my accent when I claim I've done no wrong, all the time tapping his talons on the glass rim of this chance encounter. Something glitters that may once have been mine. The school bell rings, the factory siren hoots its changing shift, and the magpie puffs up his breast, speaking with the stink of brandy and expensive cigars. He tells me he'll remember me, but he doesn't tell me why.

Workers' Playtime

Being too poor to own a car, we'd book a bus trip each bank holiday to the south west coast or, later, the Moon. The coast had donkeys and fairground rides, but the Moon had better rockpools, and Dad and I would spend hours with nets on bamboo canes, catching quick fish with bulging eyes and transparent skin, just to see their atom hearts beating before we gently lowered them back into their natural element. I'd fill my pockets with vivid shells that carried voices from deep space, patterned like galaxies, though I knew that back in my bedroom they'd be silent and dark. Most of the shops would be shut but we'd buy brittle wafers that tasted of vinegar and sea air, then strawberry ice cream in vacuum-sealed packs. We'd break even in the penny arcades, then stand on the shore that in those days seemed to stretch forever, skimming slivers of feldspar in the rough direction of Earth. We'd both doze in our seats on the way home, but I remember the retired cosmonauts singing in Russian at the back of the bus as they passed round Lunar spirit in an engraved flask. One time, Dad let me try a sip. I can still feel it burning on my tongue.

The Homing Instinct

Overnight they have carpeted the street and papered across the spaces between houses, shrinking the city to my grandparents' living room. There's a wireless in the market square, with Jack Emblow playing 'Secret Love,' and a jam jar full of coloured spills to light the fire when the weather turns. Low clouds from ribbon cut tobacco breast lavender-polished air and passing red buses glimmer like brass fire dogs. The Sun hangs from an elaborate rose. I leave my shoes at the door and my coat on the arm of an overstuffed chair, then sit in silence beneath the leaf of a folding table until I become as invisible as dropped cotton reels and forgotten birthdays, and I follow the carpet's pattern, willing abstract whorls into parrots, carriages, and a flurry of swords. There's a message. There's a map. When I blink, I am barefoot in a dried-up fountain, with traffic tumbling like china nick-nacks from a mantelpiece and birds nailed to the Town Hall walls. See how they fly. It's a long way home.

Routine Maintenance

Throughout the house there's always one lightbulb that needs fixing. Tonight, it's the spare bedroom, and although it's a long time since we've welcomed visitors – a guy we'd met in a European bar, who arrived unexpectedly with a work permit, a young son, and an entourage of stray dogs – this little box of darkness tilts the house, the street, and the whole restless city, dangerously out of kilter. I have no stepladder, so I mount a tottering ziggurat built from the books I've yet to read, and perform the neat operation, hand raised like the Statue of Liberty or The Light of the World. In the 100 watt warmth, I see that the dogs are still here, observing me shiftily from the mismatched flotsam of forgotten furniture, like schoolboys caught behind the bike sheds with cigarettes and smutty magazines. I of course have questions, but dogs are dogs and never give straight answers, and I hear the door click closed behind me as every eye avoids the skeletons – one large, one small – laid out like Pharaohs on the cheap Ikea futon.

Microwave

My uncle said you can't trust kitchens, with their gas and grease, their sugared sixpences ready to snap your teeth. He said you can't even be sure of your own hands in places like that, where there are knives and grinders, all shiny with the glint of damage. He saw it all the time when he worked in the circus: blood on the sand and hungry animals rutting sequins from the cheap fabric sky, everything stinking of sweat and frying meat. It's what the frozen-gobbed gawkers – their lips red and sticky as toffee apples – don't see that will get them in the end: the rope coiled at a glittering throat and the absence of faces beneath smudged paint. He said you can take the boy from the circus, but the circus will come looking for him; and one day it'll catch him in the kitchen, clown-eyed in the back of a burnt spoon, and all the pretty little horses with their smooth-thighed riders will be galloping the other way.

Living in the Present

A curled black cat watches black birds on a white wall: a perfect imitation of a musical score for harpsichord and violin or – close one eye and focus on nothing – a thank you note to an anonymous stranger for an unsolicited gift. The package arrived last Thursday, wrapped in starry tissue and too much tape, lighter than it looked, smelling of ozone and honeysuckle. Inside was the intricately articulated skeleton of a wren which, when it was tipped just so, sang *Thy loved ones are dreams in my dreamland*, its long, curved beak nipping each syllable as neatly as a watchmaker. There was no card, just a list of instructions for care and continuity – oil, seeds, a loving embrace, no television after 9pm – a mirror in which it can remember feathers, and a bell for it to ring each time another seaside hotel slips beneath the waves. In the mirror, a curled white cat watches white birds on a black wall: a perfect intimation of immovable property or – close the other eye and focus on what you most desire – an irreversible path between precariously stacked waves. There's singing from the doorstep and the wren rattles on its perch, its song ringing out like a harpsichord or a violin, or perhaps – block your ears and give thanks for a tissue of stars – a bell.

The White Corridor

Scraping the sun off his shoes, the man with the sea blue tie steps into the long corridor. For all its tired familiarity, it tips him off balance, like the way the land moves when you step ashore after a month at sea, the atavistic throb of engines scored into your gut and an albatross seared into your shoulders. You could flick for weeks through paint charts – Chantilly, Whisper, Bancroft, Wevet, Calm, or Simply White – but never find a name for those white walls, white lights, white shadows. The man is water as he flows past closed door after closed door, each holding a poem, a young doe dancing, a fragment of the Moon; each holding its breath. And from the far end that never ends, a woman swoops like a trapeze artist unbound, swinging from pure air alone, shuffling shapes with each swinging arc as she grows no closer, glowing in the burn of her endless transformations, trailing green like fox eyes at a garden window. And for all my tasks and promises – for he is as much me as he is you or anyone – I cannot bleach the sunlight from my footsteps or tear that baleful bird from my sunburnt back.

Adventures in Mobile Librarianship

We packed up the books again but left the furniture and the children by the road with a sign saying *Free to a Good Home*, though we couldn't say what *Home* meant, let alone what made one good or bad. We though we knew *Free*, though, and hit the road, letting the books make our choices for us, opening them at random and interpreting chance phrases as if they were tabloid horoscopes. When Gaston Phoebus told us that *in the kennel there should be a chimney to warm the hounds*, we headed for the silhouette of a factory that stood like an awkward cut-out on the horizon. When William Bottrell mentioned *monstrous head-pieces*, we turned left by an overweight man in a MAGA cap. When an anonymous Victorian ballad assured us that *The O.K. thing on Sunday is walking in the Zoo*, we stopped by a dog for want of wilder beasts. It was no way to lead a life, but no more reckless than any other, and when we ran out of road and the van broke down, rusted, and fell away from us, we used the books as stepping stones to lead us into the unknown sea. *Spirit and soul leave the old body. Fire makes everything porous and full of holes.* I sometimes wonder about the children, still sitting on a sofa at the side of the road, their tiny feet resting on a low table, reading the weather and each other's aging faces. *Out of debt, out of danger. Once upon a time. Once upon a time. Once upon a time.*

Brighter

Pages burn brighter when they contain coloured ink. It's something to do with the chemical make-up, but I don't recall the details, and the person who told me disappeared some time ago. He was near blind, but could read the connections in paper, metal and stone; knew all the languages we generally fail to acknowledge. His white cane was a divining rod that trembled across the city's veins, twitching to Wordsworth's imagined heartbeat. It was, as Böhme said, *a monstrous product of the world of darkness* (*Drey Principia*, Amsterdam, 1682), but it was a monster we believed we could pacify by feeding it our past. Now, of course, it lives in us, chewing our days to pulp, mulching them into its bulbous crop. I feel its hot breath and wonder if tattooed skin burns brighter.

Peal

Bells ring on an empty street, and it's like that point in the airport when you realise that, no, you didn't pack your own bag, but it's too late to say anything; there's a tag round the handle, it's shuffling along the belt like a mourner at its own funeral, and it's out of sight before your passport's in your pocket. Time is irregular, the hours ill-fitting in their pinched clock faces, and the bells could be a wedding or a warning, their peal like edgy laughter as the woman in the sweat-stained uniform glances the other way – remembering something her daughter said over breakfast, or a time when she herself had clutched her schoolbag to her chest and run home, her heels licked by the approaching dog of a storm – and your sharp objects and flammable liquids skate their perfect compulsory figures beneath the X-ray's tired scrutiny. In the silence that follows, the bells have left their prints on every surface, like those secret things that stranger from the bar taped to your thighs before the taxi came; the things for which they didn't know the name in English, and for which their mime suggested a wedding or a waterfall, bells echoing in an empty street, and a short, deliberate walk to a door marked *Terminal*.

Horses and Angels

On the cliff top, horses bow their heads, acknowledging the passing of angels. They remember them when they were young, flight barely hammered into their fresh feathers, glowing so bright they were almost impossible to see, their white arms coddling the lost and the dying. There were songs then, like a rainbow stroking a taut waterfall; like a moistened finger slicked on a chalice's lip; like the single pulse from the furthest star, haunting a locked observatory. From here, horses' heads are musical notes fallen from a stave, or the crooked eyes of a hundred snowmen. I hum their frozen tune as the last angel folds itself into equine dreams, becomes a grainy photograph in a local newspaper from a town washed away in last winter's floods.

Beneath

And there you are in your white shirt and ring of confidence, folding every flower in your grandmother's garden into tiny lozenges to secrete beneath your tongue. You have taken soundings of the root systems that creep beneath your lawn, beneath your house, and beneath the monsters that shelter beneath your bed: you know there are secrets deeper still, but this will do for now. As you know full well, the matter turns on an acceptance of layered notions, and the forces required to tip inertia into a sliding fall, a *Eureka!* moment of at least moral significance; yet the scent of honeysuckle makes you dizzy, and all decisions are ill-advised at this juncture. The thing is, you know there are feelings beneath facts, reactions beneath reasons, and the pollen beneath your nails will stain everything you touch more than words can possibly contain. So, you stretch into spring, bend to the first buds, fingers itching, and I wonder what is beneath your white shirt.

Unmasking

Nights line up in flat light against a grey wall, each looking hunted and each looking guilty as hell. The cop leads you in, tells you to take your time, tells you there's no need to fear, tells you he always wanted to make the world a better place, but his children are hungry and his mother's fighting for her life in a hospital on the far side of town and, really, what's a cop to do? You recognise the night immediately, its eyes still blurry with barroom lights and its pockets bulging with the last of your cash, but as you reach to place your hand on its shoulder, you notice that the next one wears the fingerprints of an ill-advised last dance, that the one after that has hair mussed crazy from leaning out a car window on a blind coast road, and that the one after that carries the song of a girl whose name you can't recall who played piano for the Sunday choir. The cop tells you once again to take your time but to make sure it's in unmarked bills, tells you he thought he could pay it all back before anyone noticed, tells you he got home to nothing but a note, children, and an unreliable microwave, that his mother deserves a decent funeral, and that sometimes ends only meet if you stretch them to almost breaking. And although you didn't notice the line break, you see that you're against the wall, surrounded by nights, each blurring into the next, each reaching out to place a guilty hand on your shoulder as the cop tells you your time's up, that anything you say will be misconstrued, and that he's only doing his job.

Please Make Up My Room

Just because they are in your handwriting doesn't mean they are necessarily your words. Likewise, just because you own a wristwatch doesn't mean your time's your own. The strap digs in in hot weather, and your muscles stiffen as you move the hotel biro through its familiar routines; but the more you think about words, the more they shed their meanings and adopt new implications. *Forever* becomes a shape glimpsed from behind in a crowded shopping mall, while *missing* is the rush of air between the spring of a diving board and the brief ecstasy of salt water. *Tomorrow* is a cinema queue as it starts to rain, or possibly a short list of whole numbers that add up differently each time you try. You have always preferred clockwork to the latest apps, but your watch is always running fast, forcing unwelcome insights into your inevitable future: you will meet a tall, dark stranger; the letter *J* will be significant; and before the cock crows three times you will have left this room forever, your pockets bulging with small bars of soap.

Highway Blues

Difficult questions push between simple gestures, so I'm careful about the way I hold the car door open, the way I hand you your keys. You never check the mirror before reversing, focusing instead on your tired eyes and immaculately dishevelled hair, while I distract myself by counting backwards from the number of miles we've travelled, rolling the radio dial as if it was a pen or an earlobe; because awkward bodies push between simple devices, so I'm careful about the way I conceptualise space, the way I negotiate proximity. You never check your speech before accelerating, focusing instead on the tension in your tired legs and immaculately dishevelled sleeves, while I distract myself by counting the number of conversations we've avoided, pecking consonants as if they were blueberries or lips; because naked truths push between innocent conversations, so I'm careful about the way I roll down the window, the way I describe the rain.

The Amputated Shadow

You are never alone, there is always the Other. Part werewolf, part conjoined twin, it occupies your skin so tightly you could not prise it away, however hard you tried. You did try once, when you first noticed it, tore yourself like wet tissue in front of your parents' mirror. You must have been about 8, the sound of the television slopping through floorboards, tears and blood spotting the carpet. It's been years since you saw it, but you know it's still there, though you can no longer remember which one's you.

King Crow

The Wanderer is a crow with staff and scrip, and a cocked hat draggled with feathers scavenged from his lesser cousins. He hop-skip-swaggers in the sick sunshine, cackling on empty cobbles like self-congratulatory applause. He's a professed believer in the locked conspiracy, a prophet of the tinfoil cap and covert handshake, though his black eye blinks like a shutter, snapping the afternoon into eighths of a second, each completely unrelated. Because, between the scenes of each advert and prognostication, he knows there is no Grand Narrative – no fundamental neo-pagan postmodernism, with all its grandsires nodding like dogs in the backs of Freudian cars – so he raps at the space with his adamant claws, caws out his clever song to all the unloved curtain twitchers, and wanders on, leaving nothing but the acid splat of half-digested half-truths, and his hollow outline in the chilly air.

Tracking

Beneath the trees, you stop like a deer that hears its whispered death, eyes brimming with amused curiosity. From time to time we've told ourselves we'll learn all nature's names, but of course we haven't, though we've collected sumptuous editions of Theophrastus, Mattioli, Linnaeus, and Miller, and we've spent hours absorbed in their meticulous illuminations, holding our breath as if they were flames we were afraid of blowing out. When I tell you that someone should paint you, you tell me that someone once did, and you unbutton your shirt to show me the pigment traces that have never washed off. Up close it looks like runes, but you tell me it's a corrupt form of Glagolitic script, and that if you squint you can see that it says *Devils cannot interfere with the stars*. I have the same tattooed in Latin on the underside of my tongue – a souvenir of a stag weekend in Sélestat in the early 1990s – but this isn't the time to tell you. Above the tallest branches, Orion whistles like an arrow for his faithful hound while, faint in scented litter, tracks like inverted hearts lead in all directions.

The Museum of Silence

In the Museum of Silence, an old man's harmonium hands rest in his lap, a hack journalist runs out of words and pricks their thumbs on empty headlines, snapped violin strings rest beneath overgrown grass, and my grandmother hangs handwashed sheets from the obliging Sun, her mouth a smile of wooden pegs. There's a chainsaw but no trees, a hammer but no wood, and an old-fashioned telephone but no one to call. There is the pressure of gentle arms and the electricity of soft hair falling across closed eyelids, but there are no words. There are never any words: neither in the confessional nor the broken-down car in the half-world in the margin of the ideal city; not even in Group, where we walk blindfold in circles, our hands on each other's shoulders, our hurt leaking from our stinging pores. In the Museum of Silence, the giftshop sells scolds' bridles and simple gags, deep scars and forgotten hymns, regrets and assumed guilt, each stamped with a logo and a warning to keep it hidden, especially from yourself. I've more than enough of this kind of stuff already, but I join the queue anyway, silently counting the coins in my pockets.

TV Times

After the scandals with the presenters – the girls, the boys, the drugs – the network decided to hire owls instead. At first there were comments, complaints, letters to Points of View, but the public adapted surprisingly fast, settling down with TV dinners to watch their wide eyes staring in studio lights, their heads bobbing like eager lawyers cutting to the nub. We all had our favourites: mine was the long eared owl on the house makeover show. As hapless couples poured their savings into loft conversions and renovations, burning cash to cook up dreams of nuclear families and lives in the country, the owl would wink like a camera's slow exposure, capturing the moments of staged drama. It was the little owls on the talk show that caught the nation's hearts, though, their quizzical zig-zag ballet upstaging even the most dazzling A-lister, flummoxing the Hollywood elite with a tip of the head, a casual hoot. They were heady days for ratings, an Indian summer for event TV, an unexpected last hurrah for the water cooler. I still have a couple of scratchily signed photos, but most people have already forgotten, their attention pin-balled by the next fad, the latest distraction. If prompted, they'd maybe recall something about bloodied wrists and revelations concerning irregular pellets, about questions in parliament, about uncomfortable silences in skeletal half-moon nights.

Breaking News

CNN is on repeat, and you are asking me again about emigration and the complex point system of individual worth. There are plus points for qualifications and expertise, for each year of verifiable experience; but there are minus points for being dead. Naturally, there are inscrutable algorithms involved, but channels of communication are open all hours, and clarification is available by instant messenger. Against economic collapse and venom in my veins, I have stockpiled antipsychotics and mood stabilisers. Against the debris from a lost light aircraft, I have a commemorative mug and a Perspex trophy for just doing my job. Against melting icecaps, I have a 12-yard swimming certificate and a book of common birds' eggs with the dust jacket missing. The weather report predicts a thaw, but you are a fantasist, constructing insubstantial assemblages from the bad news that takes your fancy, while I am a realist, sending back reports from the frontline that stretches from my head to my shaking wrist. Points stack up like skyscrapers on the other side of the world, but it's fake news and, at the bottom of the screen, the true story's already breaking.

The Newsreel Loop

A man pushes through the crowd as if it was water with a salinity of more than 35%. Barring algae, nothing's going to live in there, but this man – with his wide lapels and grey fedora, his chapped lips and amphetamine eyes – has time to kill and fish to fry: he's got flesh to strip from cold muscles and words to set in order before the situation becomes untenable. His mind's on critical mass and herd immunity; it's on a roadmap tattooed on pigskin; it's on satori, instant gratification and instant coffee; it's on hold with a synthetic melody seeping into every widening crack. A man pushes himself to the limit and then lets the invisible hand on his shoulder do the rest. He is walking on water, or sunshine, or gilded splinters; he is taking advantage of prevailing circumstances and taking issue with the ways in which his special interests are reported in mainstream media; he is reaching for the detonator at his waist, considering the plosive pleasure in *pretty please*, and chiding himself for never having firmed up that flabby belly. A man pushes his interpretation of events just a little too far, then pushes the button that thins the crowd to a watercolour wash, or to the whisper of air across razorblades.

The Debussy Bus Stop

Everything breaks sooner or later: keys, kettles, musical boxes, the clay hare on the mantelpiece. Out of habit, I carry the keys for all the houses I've left behind, and though I no longer remember which would fit which lock, there's a kind of security in the weight that presses into my thigh. I consider them as ballast as I tip slightly to pour just-boiled water on green tea, listening to the coiled melody of *Clair de Lune* as it slows like a cross-country bus at a small town where no one will get on or off. There's a café but it's closed. There's a newsstand with nothing but local papers and word searches. The engine stops but ticks with cooling as the last notes draw themselves out into everything that sounds like distance. I blow on steam and the world ripples. Through the kitchen window, a bus crosses a landscape I've only seen in sixteenth-century paintings, trucking an orchestra to another show; and out across the car park a hare waits for whatever it is that hares crave. If I could find the back door key, I'd call it over, invite it in for green tea, or just to take the weight off its slim clay legs. Sooner or later it will all break, but for now I'll wind the musical box one more time, fill my head with Debussy and roads to half-remembered houses.

Arrows

Arrows point to scenic routes, major attractions, public conveniences and transport links. There are arrows for shopping centres, and arrows for the museum, though it closed two years ago. We follow arrows to the monastery, past roadside shrines with plaster statues and plastic flowers, bowed in genuflection, that have wept all colour to the aspect of stained bone. Each map carries an arrow which points to finger-worn nothingness, polymer threads of paths and cliffs ending in dirty white: a space for renegotiating relationships and directions. Someone has scratched a heart pierced by an arrow, with angular initials tagging material space, labelling the undefined. Overhead, an aircraft, ripped from its wordless bellow, arrows its way between time zones, between imagined cities, between rough intimations of war.

Bargain

Graveyards are the new shopping malls, and I spend my Saturdays browsing their quiet aisles, comparing prices and window-shopping afterlives. My own family leaves no trace, burning used bodies like old clothes that are too worn for the charity shop, and trusting names to remembering or forgetting. As I remember this, a fresh-dug pit draws my eye, with 2-for-1 offers and loss leaders stacked in wire baskets at the entrance; so, I break the habit of a lifetime and step inside. There's a garden, and a loving god whose face is too bright to see clearly, though I'm reminded of the leaflets that some cult used hand out around the library and the Art College back in the early 70s. I can't recall their name or what they believed, but the leaflets looked like cheap comics and the face of their god was indistinctly beautiful. I remained unconvinced, but here I am in that exact paradise, nodding my head to the practised spiel of a deity dressed in beads and flared trousers, as he waves his hand towards a pastoral scene of dew-jewelled grass and lions lying down with lambs. There's my mother, knitting in the sun, and my father, with his shirt sleeves rolled up, plunging his strong arms into a clear stream. There's the car we had in the 60s, its doors open and a white blanket warm on the back seat. I ask about rest and redemption, about spreading payments, and about insurance in case of cancellation due to unforeseen circumstances. *It's all in our brochure*, the *démodé* deity assures me, pressing a leaflet of his own into my insubstantial hand. On its cover is a photograph of turned earth, and inside is a list of names printed in invisible ink.

Chuggers

The old woman at the gate asks me for spare change, while the young boy asks me for teeth. They both have buckets which they shake. The woman's bucket is blue and shaped like a castle, slightly sun-bleached on the top and one side, with traces of wet sand clinging in the angles and a shuffle of copper and silver from around the world overflowing from its turrets. The boy's bucket was made for trick or treat, a grinning plastic pumpkin, though today is any day other than Halloween, and in it are baby teeth and dog teeth, teeth with gold or zinc fillings, fossilised dinosaur teeth, and shark teeth still gripping shredded flesh. The woman's bucket sounds like wind chimes, or like a wedding, or like the end of a war, with everyone coming home. The boy's bucket sounds like teeth. The gate squeaks, but I can't tell if it's opening or closing, and I'm not sure if I really want to pass through. The woman's hands look strong for her age, hardened by years of carrying everything travellers choose to leave behind. The boy's hands look like pliers.

Outpatient

As I enter the surgery the downpour begins, a drumroll of hailstones on the flat roof. The doctor shuffles files, and I wonder why anyone still uses paper for anything other than wiping their arse or covering metaphorical cracks. In any imagined version of this scenario, there would be someone else here to recast the weather as cats, dogs, frogs, or even the Big Bad Wolf with his drumming fists and wheedling insinuations. But there's just the doctor, his face a Venetian mask and his mouth stuffed with detached calm. His lips appear to be spitting out sour milk, or counting to a million in an endangered click language, but the hailstones have grown to the size and shape of little pigs, each one squealing on impact, and a smell like barbecued flesh makes my eyes water. A nurse enters in an apiarist's veil, censing the room with cherry-scented smoke. In any imagined version of this scenario, I would weigh words and check my diary, talk things over on the short drive home. But there are no words, and there's only the Big Bad Wolf with his golf umbrella and sardonic grin, offering his elbow to lead me further into the storm.

While You Were Out

I sent you thoughts and prayers, as requested, but you were out, so they were left under the recycling bins, and the carrier mailed me a picture of your front door to reassure me about something, though I'm not sure what. The door looks different. Yes, it used to be green, and you used to keep the letter box polished, but I remember it bigger, further back from the road. I remember it open, with shopping bags, and those fluttering coloured strips to keep out flies in summer. I remember it like a weather house, with sunshades and umbrellas swinging out into days that passed like processions flanked by milk bottles jostling on cream-lipped steps, like the tri-tone chimes announcing relatives returning from fraught campaigns or expeditions to lost worlds. I rearrange cartridge shells, ammonites, a pterosaur's claw; delete all of my photographs; shape the space around my diminishing store of very best wishes.

The Ghost in the Touch

Haunting is sap in deciduous trees, is the blade that splits the pavement. When I open books, the words slip into my lap like hourglass sand, and blank pages stain my fingers. I leave my prints on cash machines, and on fairground rides where hair and voices stream in circles like magnetic fields. Ghoul or whorl: it's an impossible distinction in the clatter of machinery and 50s pop songs, in the battering of palms on boarded-up libraries. Because haunting is a coloured bulb, slowly blinking; a bird in fresh rain, slowly drinking; a reader in a darkened room, sadly thinking of all the unopened invitations that pile around him. Trees acknowledge invisible forms, act on inscrutable urges. I run my thumb along a blade of grass or steel. Haunting is a sealed envelope, the uncertain outline of a story, the narrowing space between two bodies that, like magnets, push harder away the closer they approach.

The Promise

Returning home, the lights are dim, as if someone has slackened the spectrum while we were away. Rooms are less tangible, redder and deader, and walls hint at a dull pulse. This, we decide, is what recovery looks like: not a blue dress buttoned on the first day of school; not a posey of violets in a jar by the window; not inked initials in the collar of a stiff white gown, and nothing at all like a blot-blue tarn cupped in the palm of a new-born mountain. From room to room, each lamp we light has a lower wattage than the last, so that by the time we reach the bedroom, the click of the switch plunges us into the infrared. While you fall asleep as soon as you trip, still in your outdoor clothes, onto your side of the bed, I make virtue of necessity and develop all the films that have been half-wound in cameras since the millennium, filling my lungs with vinegar as I feel lost friends and family tingle at my fingertips in gelatin and silver, with their new clothes and their eyes full of school holidays. When the day eventually dawns, I'll frame them like a medieval allegory, and tell you of all their love and in what circumstances they died; but now I'll drape you in a subtle cloth, listen to the light waves murmuring at the foot of the stairs, and wait for the robin, the thrush, the blackbird, the wren, and their whole chaotic chorus to welcome the day.

Rain Fugue

While others heard music in the rain, I always heard animal voices, urgent and arrhythmic. In the house my friend's grandfather had built on a blunt promontory, the night was kept awake by the light from distant factories, the urgent business of insects deep in the mattress. Paperbacks with lurid covers lined the walls: cheap Pan thrillers from the 70s, chaste romances, memoirs by astronomers and archaeologists. Incomplete packs of playing cards offered a Tarot of sorts, though we ignored their predictions as the storm bundled like bears across the roof, grunting and spitting, murmuring its hunger. In the bright morning, a stranger stood on the lawn, naked but for a dead bear, huge upon her shoulders. When she spoke, we didn't understand a word, but the clouds in her eyes cried in the language of our aching loins.

The Elephant in the Room

I leave reminders in every room: notes, knotted string, and special keepsakes. They tell me why I'm there, but not why I'm here, not why some things matter and some things don't. They remind me that it's a time of tree pollen and big cities, of sporting fixtures and airline disasters, and that trees are taking over the cities, sport is just for empty seats and sex dolls, and our conception of disaster is being recalibrated with each Xeroxed broadside slipped under the front door. For all the reminders, I forget anniversaries and other deadlines, forget to eat or shave, but on two out of three days I remember that the figures at the periphery of my vision are nothing but mild hallucinations. Somewhere amongst the uncollected bottles and tickets for cancelled flights, there's a road map for recovery, though I can't remember from what, or where I am on its straight, featureless highways. Of course, there's an elephant in the room but, even as I forget how to write or tie knots, I'm reluctant to wake it from its fitful sleep.

Freeze

When all calls freeze, I step into the garden, brushing through waist-high grass and flowering weeds. I sit on the wall and think about caves and seashells, about the point at which the mouth becomes the interior, and how sooner or later everything becomes sand. I'm idly curious about how big an oasis needs to be before it's no longer just a part of the desert, and I wonder if the Earth's really big enough to consider itself as anything other than a part of space. A gust of wind fills the air with dandelion parachutes, and when they clear I see that the elephant has joined me, grey as cigar ash and plump as a lung. The elephant has no first-hand experience but remembers hearing about the Al-Ahsa Oasis in Saudi Arabia, which covers more than thirty square miles and has more than a quarter of a million palm trees. I can't get my head around that sort of number, so the elephant tells me to imagine a palm tree at each mile between here and the Moon. It's no harder than seeing crabs or bulls in random stars, and I add a few monkeys for colour and light relief, which the elephant views with the same affection as I do. We both feel small, and my mind turns back to the niceties of distinctions between species. A monkey snatches a garden gnome from the undergrowth and races back to the trees, and I finish a mug of tea I have no recollection of making. When the moment freezes, I walk into the waist-high house, light the small cigar I have saved for a time like this, and lock myself in an elephant-shaped room.

Maintaining a Routine

I root out time like a pig snuffling for truffles, troubling the soil for unlikely treasures. I measure time like a surveyor on a bombsite, sighting lines, recording precise dips and pitches, itching to level the land. I capture time like a wasp in a wineglass, sealed with a holiday postcard with no address or message but a first class stamp. This, I decide, is enough similes, so I sit down with time, brew us both tea, and fetch the best biscuits in the Golden Jubilee tin. At first there's an awkward silence, but as I sip my tea my words loosen, and for some reason I tell time about playing pool thirty years ago and potting the last two balls with my eyes closed; and then I remember a friend and I tunnelling beneath a deckchair on a north Devon beach, so that when his mother sat in it, it fell in, pitching her legs towards flapping gulls. But time's not listening, because it was there and remembers it all better than I do. And time adjusts its theodolite, noting the lines that connect upturned earth and an upturned wineglass, the neat angles of white, red and black on baize, an upturned deckchair and the tide wandering in to flatten sand. There are crumbs on the carpet, unsightly stains in empty cups, and the room smells of sea air and mushrooms. I switch on the TV, change my mind, then switch it off again.

A Census of Preconceptions

No test is perfect. Lights flicker like wings on the edge of heaven and journalists rake through ashes at the foot of a dormant volcano. There are points to be raised about rights and privileges, scores to be apportioned for elegance and grace, and reports to be written concerning adaptation to twenty-first century mores. Whoever's responsible has appointed an unbiased panel of three witches and three wise monkeys, furnished them with cauldrons and bananas, and fitted them all with radio mics and body-cams. They're forbidden to speak to reporters but can't resist dropping broad hints and banana skins to be paraded for the public once the ashes have been washed off. Preliminary analysis suggests a spike in shape-shifting, though this should not be mistaken for social mobility, and demonisation rates remain more-or-less constant. Levitation is the new normal – with or without wings – and light bends itself like a retired acrobat. No test is perfect and every day presents fresh problems, but trends are encouraging if we maintain a sense of decorum and keep believing in our regimen of placebos.

Hold the Front Page

A brown briefcase spills leaves, and the pavement's thick with newspapers. The world is tired of keys and combinations, so it rips the front from all reports and affidavits, peeling down to their pith and juice. News breaks so often that it's frightened to get out of bed, and the unwary are elbowed to oblivion by newshounds and paparazzi, lucky if they spot themselves naked and misspelled in a column on page 58. Insult or injury: lawyers chase ambulances, police cars and ice cream vans; anything with a bell is fair game for compensation. And by the road, that briefcase fills with rain; fills with young boys bombing, and with escapologists struggling in the chains their lovers locked before they walked away. All policies are null and void as, in brown water scudded with brown leaves, headlines rewrite themselves as myths, and Orpheus dons mask and flippers, his lyre warped, his strings rusty.

The Evolutionary Urge

When we stopped wearing watches, our hands became lighter: a small point, but that's the nature of evolution – one day you're a fish, then before you know it, you're shopping for trousers, considering colour, cut, and the ethical sourcing of material. Or perhaps you are a lemur, developing digits to suit specific circumstances, whether that's riddling out grubs from deep beneath tree bark, or forming barre chords to ease your way into a Status Quo tribute act. So, when we stopped wearing watches, it wasn't just our hands that became lighter, but also our spirits and the pigmentation of our eyes, until we floated above ourselves, timeless, observing the earth and its deep, disordered waters as if through a glass, darkly, our hearts strumming that good ol' 12-bar blues.

Pulse

Just when it seems like silence, you notice the bass. It's in the water running under the floorboards that you didn't think you could hear, and it's in the gas, the electric and the fibre-optics that you didn't think made a noise. It's in the cat's throat when he stops purring, and in the lawnmower as it's swallowed by weeds. It's the ache in your jaw after the tooth's gone, and the ache of familiar scent in confined spaces. It's John Entwistle carving mountains with four fingers and a thumb, and Holger Czukay hammering one note for a whole show, just because. It's the kick-drum of insects that you feel in your stomach, and the grind of the Earth's machine heart turning. It's the sleeping beast that swallows all words and, just when you think you have grasped its rhythm, it is silence.

A Folktale for Every Occasion

The building is empty as a well, so I shout for the help I'm too embarrassed to ask for when anyone's home, relieved when no-one comes running. There's a numbered list of actions In Case of Emergency, and though it would be hard to frame this afternoon as an emergency, I follow them, just in case, dialling 999 on a bad line and assembling myself in the car park, like flat-pack furniture with impenetrable diagrams and poorly translated instructions. We're miles from the sea, so by the time the coastguard arrives, clammy in his oilskins, my thumbs are blistered from Allen keys, but I look complete to the casual eye. He anchors the launch he has dragged from Scarborough, throws a lifebelt over my head with his first shot, winning a goldfish in a bag full of tap water. We look at each other, each acknowledging parts well played. The goldfish's lips are moving, so I loosen the neck of the bag to hear. *Go back to your empty life*, it says in a voice that echoes from the bottom of a well, *there's nothing to see here*.

Traces

I step outside for smoke, but there's only steam rising from spilt coffee and a rough sketch of breath still hanging around from old conversations. While I was out of work, I learned to read such traces, so I know that there was a man – 56 years old, 5' 9" – with brown shoes and a voice that squeaked like a windmill in need of oil. He works in retail, selling stationery and craft supplies in an out-of-town mall, and once, when he was a child of 7 or 8, a heron flew in through his bedroom window and stood at the foot of his bed. Years later he got a tattoo of a heron on his right forearm, though a lot of people he meets assume it's a stork or a crane. A bird is a bird is a bird. Looking closer, I see that he was talking to a taller woman whose head was shaved like an egg. She plays piano on cruise ships, though there has been no work for a year or more. She, too, was once visited by the same heron, and has an identical tattoo, though her more ornithologically aware circle of friends and acquaintances generally identify the King of the Birds. They both gave up smoking on the same day in 1997, but the steam from the coffee tells me that neither of them knew any of this about the other, and they only spoke of problems finding parking spaces in a city of this size. Away to the west, a finger of smoke tickles the sky, sketching the outline of a bird.

Fathoming

When we stopped sleeping together, I moved into the bathysphere, nesting myself against the pressure. The light changes at these depths, all warmth lost, and I watch you at breakfast through fused quartz, your movements doubled and distorted as you mash sardines onto cold toast, grimace at sour coffee. On the backs of old greetings cards, I map the unexplored geography of insubstantial foundations, tracing subtle contours for pitch and fall, while documenting seepage and slippage on hand-held Super 8. Each evening I file lengthy reports, seal copies in wine bottles and release them to irascible tides. It keeps me busy, and I barely notice you leave, like the first tiktaalik aspiring to dry land.

Population: 0

Normal is the town at the bottom of the hill, backing onto the sea. It's the whitewashed pub and the post office closed for lunch, and it's the row of chapels converted to holiday lets. It's the railway embankment that ends in empty space, and the archive of proposed developments subject to funding bids. I remember Normal when it was nothing but sandcastles and donkeys in straw hats, when there was nothing to eat but lurid ices, and we worked ten-hour shifts building barques from wooden lolly sticks. I saw it shrink as politicians packed their navies into glass bottles, leaving them to gather dust behind the bar in the old boys' clubs; and I remember visiting for the funeral of the last living inhabitant, her coffin lost beneath swathes of wreaths, while home movies stuttered along dockyard walls, filling in for family and friends. As far as I know, Normal may have been ironed flat in the last war, or stolen away by the sea, but when I stop late at that lay-by before the last hill, all the stars are where they used to be, and the red call box glows on the darkened verge. Everything looks normal, but I know better than to answer when the phone rings.

The Inconstant Babysitter

The pause before thunder brings me home, helps me off with my coat and my shoes. It makes me a coffee while I sit, not paying attention to the television that I don't remember turning on. There's something heavy in my trouser pocket, something unfamiliar about the arrangement of chairs and ornaments, and I feel there's something I need to set straight before the storm releases its unequivocal applause. Upstairs, the children dodge sleep, and talk in loud whispers about unfinished homework and schoolyard crushes; and although I know that there are no children – there never were – their excited chatter's reassuring, like an astronaut's thin umbilical, tethering life to life. Before I drift off, I hear the pause before thunder, feel its solicitous breath against my ear. The coffee's cold, my mouth's sour, the television is a stolen car reversing through a shop window, and all the absent children are crying for glasses of water.

Homes under the Hammer

You are tidying the kitchen, stacking cans, nesting pans inside each other, and breaking crockery with a small hammer before placing the fragments in biscuit tins and taping them shut. I don't know why, but I remember you saying something about moving, something about a longer life through discipline, and something about omens deep in the feathers of the birds that gather at the back door for scraps. You are crushing fruit, pulses and raw vegetables into the gaps between floorboards, washing them down with coffee and smoothing them over with a wooden spoon. And here I am, in the attic or the cellar I didn't even know we had, listening to the bottles and glasses ringing their ice cube tunes as if from miles away, scrabbling amongst stuffed suitcases for the right words, slapping the walls in darkness as I feel for a latch or at least a light switch. You tidy the kitchen until there's nothing left, then you start on the bathroom, grinding the fittings to dust, then sticking stamps on each ceramic tile and posting them to creditors, debtors, and all our past addresses.

Slick

There's a lipstick smack on a cracked cup, a tower of dishes stacked up on the draining board I sat on, aged seven, for my father to scrub oil from my feet. In south-east Cornwall life slows down, the brochures claim, but in each dipped plate, another disaster in folk memory rises to scare the lost boys who slipped between wars or, at least, well-thumbed pages. Shipwrecked Swallows and abandoned Amazons lie like tired seals on a jetty that sways above a weedy sea, its purpose forgotten. There's a mermaid on an eggcup, a sailor on a spoon, their romance remembered in the clink of steel on cheap china, the wink as he dips inside her, the plump rainbows of oil and soap, washing away, washing away. And I think of south-west Devon in the spring of '67: birds black and sightless, the stains on my skin, impossible shapes and numbers reconfiguring themselves in tourist attractions and on the teatime news, the cold hard press on the backs of my legs, the almost scalding water. Patterns wash from plates, sailors were never found, oil still bleeds through greedy fingers, and the mermaid was only ever a fish, far out at sea, rainbow-haloed in soap or oil. There's a lipstick smack on a cracked cup. I'll leave it there.

Sawing Ourselves in Half

I store my selves in a conjuror's case, while hers are stacked with party dishes, dripping drops of misspent nights, each more sweet than the last. Like a dog-eared pack, we lie on the grass between cups and capes, sleights and tricks that tick into each other. Wands bloom to warm flowers, stretched with skin, slipped beneath seed trays in a glass pavilion, where metaphors dodge each other before completion. Back in the kitchen, the kettle whistles a pure A, pulls hares from hats, steams the paper from the ceiling, revealing traits and foibles labelled with strangers' names.

The Armchair Volcanologist

Before he moved out, the previous owner hid a volcano in the house, leaving cryptic clues in the title deeds and red herrings hanging from blatant hooks in all the bedrooms. The survey showed nothing and the estate agent kept mum, though her eyes almost gave the game away as I signed the contract with a quill plucked from the albatross that had circled my steps for years; but when I set the herrings free – carefully unthreading their breath from cruel steel and lowering them like paper submarines into a river I conjured from sweat and childhood memories – I could smell the sulphur, hear deep growling in an elemental gut. Following my Boy Scout training, I lifted floorboards, tapping along each planed edge to loose stray landscapes. I stretched my arm up unswept chimneys until my fingers felt sky, and down drains until I reached the sea, with its shoals of herring, its sigh and swell. I peeled off wallpaper, then plaster, then bricks, crushing them fine as sifted sand, leaving nothing but a flaky skin of render and rumour between myself and tutting neighbours. There's an albatross on the roof, the lurid hook of his beak scraping like tired boots in an exercise yard. He tells me not to worry, that he lived here an eternity before me, and that I should rest my hot stone emptiness before it erupts.

Swarm

Bodies break up every day, but still we're surprised when it happens to us, and we struggle for an appropriate image. Let's try this for size: a beehive in a golden field, the Sun low, and a pandemonium of urgent buzzing. There's honey fit for gods and wax to light lovers to that room where nothing is understood and nothing is forgotten. These are some of our days and dreams, but what of all the bees? Fifty, maybe sixty, thousand points of coming, going, and unquestioned giving; each unique but indistinguishable in birth, death, and the perfect work in between, until one day they're nothing but an illustration in a school textbook or a painting with a doubtful provenance that tourists pass without looking on their way to the Bosch or the Leonardo. This is who we are, standing in this mess of a cluttered kitchen, not knowing what to do with our hands or the rest of our lives, as millions of cells die or divide in a constant buzz of breaking. We only sting when we're afraid, and there's sweetness at the heart of our shattering.

Primary Healthcare

The hospital always keeps its distance, hanging on the other side of town, somewhere across the motorway. However we approach, it's always the wrong direction, and signs swing like turbines, generating misdirection as traffic builds up and the Sun stops overhead, bleaching all the colour from car bonnets and from the awnings of shops that haven't changed hands since the last war, whenever that was. It's been so long that our snapped bones have knit into inefficient angles, our hearts have become accustomed to irregular beats. We make do without breathing. As the one-way system sweeps us away, we pass a glass coach with black horses, black plumes lolling and blinkered against uncomfortable histories. Inside is a garden where a familiar child whose name no-one can remember plucks peas from a vine, opening pods like newspapers or a Bible.

Not Fade Away

Skeleton sits, drumming his knuckles on a closed book, that Bo Diddley beat of blunt bones. It's a Bible night, a tribal night: a night when the dead come back to rap on the shutters and shake the shingles, raise the roof and lower the temperature to cool, cool, cool. It's a piano night, with keys clacking like loose wooden tongues that gossip and kiss by the light of a black moon that perches like an owl on a lightning-blasted tree. Skeleton sits, humming beehive vamps to the snare drum scratch of beetles in the boardwalks and bedposts, riffing honey into all those sticky places we've been told not to touch. It's a feast night, a beast night; a *so-good-to-meet-you, so-good-to-eat-you, little piggy, little piggy* night, with thick poppy breath and white teeth teasing hot, soft skin. And skeleton sits, rattling those rhythms like rolling dice, with snake eyes hooded and impossible to resist. It's a tasty night, a wasted night: a night to shimmy and shudder to the stuttering flutter of bone on slack catgut. Bare feet shuffle on bare boards. *Come a little closer. Come a little closer.* Skeleton winks, and the teeth in an old skull sweat.

Heat

Nights when you wake up with summer's sticky hand too familiar with the parts of your body that are no one else's business. You've been drinking – or you haven't been drinking enough – and your head's swimming with the useless ceiling fan as you reach for the sheet that's rucked on the floor. It's been too hot since the late 60s and the air knows all your sensitive places, just as the standby light on the TV has borne witness to a catalogue of indiscretions that will always stick in your throat, however solicitous professional listeners may appear. Regardless of temperature, sleep demands weight – a duck down counterpane that stifles your breath, an arm round your waist like a snake on a medieval altarpiece, or a tongue that tastes the salt at the nape of your neck – and even the ribbons bound round your wrists can't tether you now. You need a drink or a doctor, and your head's buzzing with the insects that will flay you before morning. The hands over your ears are not your own, and summer's lips are dripping with the promises you fall for every time.

The Isolation Waltz

For a long time, my heart was a schoolroom with gas lamps and iron benches, with low light painting each surface in pastel chalks. I turned at the jangle of a dropped gold locket containing a snip of baby hair or a wisp of northern fog. There was a woman in a starched blue dress, with blue hair and blue lips, whose face and fingers were coral and whose feet were wrapped in iron. She held a chest the colour of a tiger's eye, winking, and told me that she was a fan of improvisation and that I was in a high-risk category. In the stillness that followed, traffic passed between the songs of blackbirds and my cheap alarm clock rattled. A dog barked. When she offered me the box, it smelled of old library books and in my hand it felt like a label I couldn't unpick from a cheap office chair. As I watched, the box opened itself, and inside was my heart and a photograph of five young men strolling down Broadway back in the 1970s. I took my heart and stepped into the picture to the sound of a C harmonica, and there, over on the sidewalk, in the shadow of the Empire State Building, was a dropped gold locket. I stooped to pick it up, but it was as heavy as floorboards. I closed my eyes and saw a green pool in a dark wood, and all I could hear was a stranger from the South with a funeral on his mind, reminding me that I had a class in less than an hour. His voice sounded like frogs.

Loving the Perseids

When he comes home late, he smells of meteors, their scent clinging to his face and fingers. It's like wax and oranges, or the crushed field after the circus has departed, with its candyfloss clutter churned in the paw prints and tyre tracks. He carries the burn of broken comets like a lover's handprints on the curve of his shoulder, the pinch of his waist. The idea of light makes him dizzy and, when he closes his eyes, fragments of every narrative he has ever trusted vaporise at 36 miles per second. The house is asleep, along with everyone in it, and he walks from moonlit room to moonlit room, between the beds of all the people he never grew up to be, trailing haze from the Kármán Line. One of these nights a child will wake for just a moment, watch him burn up, and will have forgotten by the morning.

Out of Town

Beyond the range of church bells, time follows its own instincts, sniffing round the bins and leaving scent marks on parked vans. It trots across the spaces between wire fences and portacabins, with a look in its eye that says there's nothing to see here – move along. When you turn off the light after a long shift, time is the shape you catch through the window, briefly rippling the darkness; and when you tip your empties into the recycling bin, it's every sound that isn't breaking glass. In windswept warehouses and the over-lit waiting rooms of car showrooms and new surgeries that are impossible to reach by public transport, there are posters of church bells featuring motivational slogans and emergency numbers, and the looped music in the Tesco Express has an almost familiar ring; but there have been no church bells here since the Dark Ages – though here, amongst the broken glass and magazines, time does what it damn well likes, and it could still be the Dark Ages for all anyone can tell.

The Coming of the Comet

Comet trails of fragmented nursery rhymes abrade the sky, close enough to touch, though you decide not to for fear of burning your fingers. Whatever happened to the ducks who never came back? Why was it so important to that spider to make it up the spout, and how did it feel when, rain-shivered and exhausted, it blinked in the bathroom light? These are things you think you should know, should have understood when parents, siblings and teachers repeated them over and over until you were word perfect. But like Perceval before the Fisher King, you never asked the right question, never even suspected that there was a question. And now there are portents in the eastern dark, flaming like dragons, demanding that you step in and do something where all the king's horses and all the king's men have failed time and time again, and that you find that little piggy wherever he's hiding and make him face up to his responsibilities. And you nearly reach up to grab hold of something, but all the people who bow like worms in the church with the steeple turn their blank faces to you, as the Grail procession passes, the red dragon writhes with the white, and the sky turns brittle as burnt books.

The Gift Shop is Currently Closed

The heart's an untidy sundial in a museum of artificial light. There are chemical reactions and the predictable chaos of waves, mirrors acknowledging mirrors until they vanish, and the glow you kindle by combing the right words through silence. There are clouds with Latin names in varying states of *déshabillé*, blackout blinds, and discreet turnings away from disaster or desire, each illuminated by sparks struck by breath on a freshly-cleaned window; and there are life-size replicas of dreamless sleep and the far side of the Moon, with nothing but a plastic torch to find your way back out. Occasionally, the beam will catch a masked attendant painting out the windows or sweeping away stray threads from the Sun, and they'll raise their thumb and mumble about dark, dark times. The guidebook is all ink and no paper, and what sounds like a heartbeat is probably someone nailing the last door shut. In spite of this location, the sundial has never skipped a second, even making adjustments for daylight saving and night-time profligacy, though no one has ever witnessed the exact point of the lost or gained hours.

Birdsong 101

In the last few minutes, the cat has curled himself into unobtrusive cushions, the Sun has fingered the edges of bookshelves, the postman has slipped nothing through the letterbox, and a thrush has settled at the open window. It chortles in its throat, lascivious as wet gardens, and carries the sky in its eye like a framed eclipse. *The source of art is love*, it says, quoting Hockney, its heart drum-thumping under its hipster waistcoat. And I know it's true, because in the last few minutes, I've checked my email a dozen times, sketched the cat on a post-it note, remembered an ekphrastic poem in a paperback with an orange spine, and imagined a bird that would settle at the open window, telling me just what I need to hear.

Slapstick

In line with our green agenda, we replaced the TV with a Punch and Judy show and a fortune teller. It was weird at first, with soaps and home improvement shows alike ending in comic carnage, but within weeks it felt like every voice we'd ever heard had had that rasping burr, and that the prize for every daytime quiz had always been a string of contested sausages. On the hour, the lights dimmed and a made-up man in Victorian gypsy drag came by to prognosticate on the next day's weather and the rise and fall of waves of plague and disaster capitalism. We took him to task on respect and appropriation, but he explained that he was a bankrupt hotelier with a wife, three children, and a modest petting zoo to feed, and that cultural integrity didn't feed the goats, so we cut him slack and had to admit he made the role his own. We nominated him for a BAFTA, but never heard back. Meanwhile, the puppeteer did what he could, taking on everything from the Olympics to classic movies with his wooden archetypes, and we roared as the policeman romped home in the 1500 meters and our stoic eyes glistened with Mr Punch as Judy and the dog turned away on that foggy Casablanca airstrip. It was as if, stripped of big budgets and facial expressions, we saw the stories for the first time, their pain and passion raw as a slapped cheek. And when Punch pranced on as a swazzle-gobbed Prime Minister, we roared at the nonsense and the perfect comic timing, squeaking along with the catchphrases and bawling *Oh no it's not!* at each outrageous fib.

You'd think it would wear thin but, more than a year on, here we are, crossing palms with silver, checking our temperatures and our waterproof jackets, and whooping at the painted fool. *Here comes the policeman! Here comes the crocodile! That's the way to do it!*

Crisis Management

When the ghosts won't leave, I phone the Crisis number I carry for such emergencies. When they ask how many, I explain that windows and mirrors are one and the same, and that all my reflections are just a little out of sync. There are ears pressed to the other sides of all surfaces. When they ask how long this has been going on for, I tell them about the drawer full of stopped watches and the sundial in the cellar that keeps perfect time. The fingers drumming on the chair arm are not mine. When they ask me to rate intensity on a scale of 1 to 10, I describe the first time I saw limbs and faces in trees, and how even silence chants its own confessions. The head in my lap could be a dog or a devil, but I'm afraid to open my eyes. When they ask me to call a cab and check myself in as a matter of urgency, I tell them I can't find my birth certificate, I can't find my phone, and the only map I own shows bomb damage to my hometown after the last war. A large black bird spars with its shadow on the scuffed wooden floor. When they ask why I am speaking to an empty room, I can't answer.

The Gleaning

Breathless, I am still waiting for flood or fire. It's been a biblical summer, with frogs and fevers, pulpits and pronouncements, and now the leaves are turning apostate, renouncing all creeds. If I were my grandmother, I'd hedge my bets with prayers and playing cards, pebbles tied in silk, and a horseshoe nailed to the back door lintel; I'd argue the toss with doorstep evangelists and shoeshine boys; and I'd gather warm bread in my floral apron to feed the starving millions. If I were my father, I'd bite my tongue until it bled truth, build an ark or a fallout shelter from scraps stored in the old washhouse, then set the world on my strong, blunt shoulders, that tiny bit closer to the Sun. If I ever become myself again, I'll put my trust in words and weathervanes, in boats and buckets, in brass barometers and birds that congregate on washing lines; I'll weigh apocalypse and apocrypha and wait out the fury of flood and fire; then, I'll still my breath and listen to what the leaves say on their long, long journey to the ground.

imdb

I've changed the locks and changed my mind, tidied away the ballpoint pens and old headphones. The house is too small for bad music, and my arm's a sketched web of phone numbers I'll never ring. I dreamed last night of steam trains and a wooden cabin in the middle of a city – maybe Paris or Chicago – where I met a school friend after forty years. He heated a kettle on a single gas ring, telling me about one time that he met my mother in a dentist's waiting room, where they talked about the copies of *Horse and Hound* piled by the fish tank. How can you believe in a dentist who's into blood sports? I woke up thinking about Dustin Hoffman, wondering how convincing I'd be in drag, and trying to remember if he's ever had a singing role in a musical. I consider Googling it, but get distracted and order a set of screwdrivers, a Bluetooth speaker system, and box of cheap pens.

Epiphanies for All

In the absence of clear government guidelines, I've convinced myself that angels are everywhere, offering certainty, reliable advice and, when I need it, a firm hand on my shoulder that just says I'm doing ok. Usually they're invisible, so I need to close my eyes to see them, slim and magnificent as a Doré engraving; other times they'll take the earthly form of a traffic warden or a daytime game show host. I don't know what I'm doing with my life so, as MPs sweat and bluster, harrumphing in the blowback from a million avoidable tragedies, I seek the comfort of catchphrases and fixed penalty notices, parking my car on the double yellows outside the studio and hammering on their pearly gates. *No deal*, says a disembodied voice. *For you the chase is over*. It's what I need and, reassured, I return to the ecclesiastical gloom of my ticket-plastered car. There's a tap on the windscreen, another fixed fine, and angel in the back seat reminds me that I'm the weakest link. On the radio, the Minister for Innovation and Obfuscation promises epiphanies for all, free school lunches, and wings by next Easter at the latest. I'd head for home, but even the road markings are too ambiguous to trust.

Keep Calm and Carry a Reminder

When I try to grasp instructions, they slip from my fingers like wet balloons, and when I try to take in the warnings, they just shuffle on the step, awkward as carol singers turning up in July. That's the problem with verbs and their verifications: the vertiginous shifts of perspective as they flash from figurative to literal, and thence to littoral, littering the shore, unsure of their equivocal relationship to the real. When I try to reel in the years, they tug on the line like abandoned shopping trolleys, and when I pinpoint root causes, they squirm like worms in a school laboratory. It's a labour of love in a layby on the A303, somewhere south-west of Amesbury: *amo, amas, amat* – I'm at the end of my tether, together with a host of fallen comrades, fallen angels, and fallen leaves. There are instructions nailed to supermarket doors and slipped under windscreen wipers under cover of night. *Exite, Leave*: a thrill and a threat, a page turned, lives unfathomable as blind fish. I grasp my mother's pen as if it was a wax baby, my finger and thumb closing in a neat ellipse the shape of a mummy's eye. I try to understand but can't even stand, but if at first I don't succeed, I'll suck on the seeds until green sprouts from my split lips.

Footnote

History spreads out like a coarse sheet, smelling of cough sweets and fresh bandages. It's tucked in tight to the corners of our everyday lives, pulled up almost to our eyes. Though no one sleeps, we lie in a neat row like the seven dwarfs, though two metres apart. When I stare at the ceiling, I see mountains in the stippled anaglypta, a river valley with deer stooping to drink beneath a sky untroubled by human settlers or vapour trails. Of course, it's all subjective, and others may see the clipped fleece of a white alpaca, or the rumoured Russian crash landing on the Moon; because this is history we're talking about, and every footnote is a ripe red herring hanging from an indigenous spear, queering the official account. Sooner or later darkness will come and interpretation will be less important, but the night will be cough sweets and bandages, and history will still pin us where we lie.

Off-Peak Single

The turnstile jammed, trapping me half way through, casting me in the role of inconvenience for the queue that gathered in Fibonacci curves, bristling with smartphones and resentment. I scanned and inserted my ticket at every possible angle, then the same angles again but in a different order, but the gate didn't move and the crowd swelled, became unruly, pleading and threatening. On the other side, the hall had emptied, fallen to silence as the lights went out. My ticket wore thin, and when I lifted it to my eye I could see through it to the desperate, angry, Biblical mass who looked to me for the release of all their earthly cares, or at least for loaves and fishes. By the time the ticket had fallen to fine powder, the turnstile was thick with moss, with small shrubs chancing their tentative lives in this emerging world. Bees waggled their stories of new terrain, and a yellow songbird scored its eloquent truth. My hands throb with the primal power of mulch and loam, my fingers unfolding in the prestidigitation of new life. I regret to inform you of the cancellation of all services. Let there be light.

Debrief

Afterwards, he was asked what he was thinking. *There were reports*, he said, *of capacities and measures, of influences and communities, of governments and unnecessary long-haul flights. But what I thought was: normal laughter, singing out of tune, and praise for all the cleaners, because cleanliness trumps godliness every single time.* Afterwards, he was asked what he was feeling. *I felt*, he said, *the uneasy sway of railway carriages switching points, the precipitous temperature drop as the Sun passed behind the Moon, the gut-deep rumble of thunder overhead, and of food disappearing from shelves.* Afterwards, he was asked what he dreamed. *I dreamed*, he said, *of trees with blunt fingers and stars with sharp edges, of a familiar city that grows every time I close my eyes; and I dreamed that everyone who had ever cared for me was alive and skipping down concrete steps leading to the sea. Everyone was smiling*, he said. *Everyone was smiling.*

Selected Poetry Titles Published by SurVision Books

Seeds of Gravity: An Anthology of Contemporary Surrealist Poetry from Ireland
Edited by Anatoly Kudryavitsky
ISBN 978-1-912963-18-8

Invasion: An Anthology of Ukrainian Poetry about the War
Edited by Tony Kitt
ISBN 978-1-912963-32-4

Noelle Kocot. *Humanity*
(New Poetics: USA)
ISBN 978-1-9995903-0-7

Marc Vincenz. *Einstein Fledermaus*
(New Poetics: USA)
ISBN 978-1-912963-20-1

Helen Ivory. *Maps of the Abandoned City*
(New Poetics: England)
ISBN 978-1-912963-04-1

Tony Kitt. *The Magic Phlute*
(New Poetics: Ireland)
ISBN 978-1-912963-08-9

John W. Sexton. *Inverted Night*
(New Poetics: Ireland)
ISBN 978-1-912963-05-8

Afric McGlinchey. *Invisible Insane*
(New Poetics: Ireland)
ISBN 978-1-9995903-3-8

Michelle Moloney King. *Another Word for Mother*
 (New Poetics: Ireland)
 ISBN 978-1-912963-31-7

Matthew Geden. *Fruit*
 (New Poetics: Ireland)
 ISBN 978-1-912963-16-4

Clayre Benzadón. *Liminal Zenith*
 (New Poetics: USA)
 ISBN 978-1-912963-11-9

Thomas Townsley. *Tangent of Ardency*
 (New Poetics: USA)
 ISBN 978-1-912963-15-7

Mikko Harvey & Jake Bauer. *Idaho Falls*
 (Winner of James Tate Poetry Prize 2018)
 ISBN 978-1-912963-02-7

Anton Yakovlev. *Chronos Dines Alone*
 (Winner of James Tate Poetry Prize 2018)
 ISBN 978-1-912963-01-0

Tony Bailie. *Mountain Under Heaven*
 (Winner of James Tate Poetry Prize 2019)
 ISBN 978-1-912963-09-6

Charles Kell. *Pierre Mask*
 (Winner of James Tate Poetry Prize 2019)
 ISBN 978-1-912963-19-5

Jon Riccio. *Eye, Romanov*
 (Winner of James Tate Poetry Prize 2020)
 ISBN 978-1-912963-24-9

Aoife Mannix. *Alice under the Knife*
  (Winner of James Tate Poetry Prize 2020)
  ISBN 978-1-912963-26-3

Alison Dunhill. *As Pure as Coal Dust*
  (Winner of James Tate Poetry Prize 2020)
  ISBN 978-1-912963-23-2

Becki Hawkes. *The Naming of Wings*
  (Winner of James Tate Poetry Prize 2021)
  ISBN 978-1-912963-34-8

Charles Borkhuis. *Spontaneous Combustion*
  (Winner of James Tate Poetry Prize 2021)
  ISBN 978-1-912963-30-0

Ciaran O'Driscoll. *Angel Hour*
  ISBN 978-1-912963-27-0

Tim Murphy. *The Mouth of Shadows*
  ISBN 978-1-912963-29-4

George Kalamaras. *That Moment of Wept*
  ISBN 978-1-9995903-7-6

George Kalamaras. *Through the Silk-Heavy Rains*
  ISBN 978-1-912963-28-7

Anton G. Leitner. *Selected Poems 1981–2015*
  Translated from German
  ISBN 978-1-9995903-8-3

Order our books from http://survisionmagazine.com/bookshop.htm

L - #0074 - 201222 - C0 - 210/148/4 - PB - DID3453642